# peak two part 2

Alan Brighouse
David Godber
Peter Patilla

Nelson

**Thomas Nelson and Sons Ltd**
Nelson House   Mayfield Road
Walton-on-Thames   Surrey KT12 5PL

51 York Place
Edinburgh   EH1 3JD

**Thomas Nelson (Hong Kong) Ltd**
Toppan Building 10/F   22A Westlands Road
Quarry Bay   Hong Kong

Distributed in Australia by
**Thomas Nelson Australia**
480 La Trobe Street
Melbourne   Victoria 3000
and in Sydney, Brisbane, Adelaide and Perth

Filmset in the Nelson Teaching Alphabet
by Mould Type Foundry Ltd
Leyland   Preston   England

Printed and bound in Great Britain by
Ebenezer Baylis & Son Ltd   Worcester and London

**Design**   Sharon Platt, Linda Reed
**Photography**   Chris Ridgers
**Illustration**   Taurus Graphics, David Farris,
David Mostyn, Paul Stickland
Photographic props courtesy of E J Arnold

Items on page 59 by kind permission of J Sainsbury plc.

# Contents

# Number

What must be added to each of these to make 100?

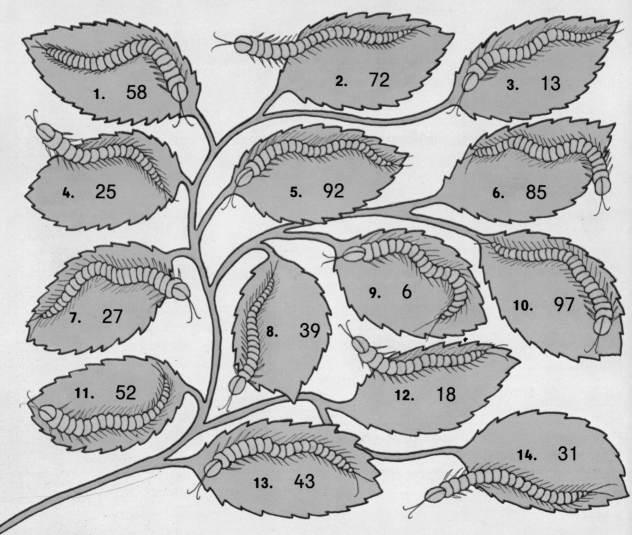

1. 58
2. 72
3. 13
4. 25
5. 92
6. 85
7. 27
8. 39
9. 6
10. 97
11. 52
12. 18
13. 43
14. 31

Add 99 to each of these numbers.

15. 16    16. 125    17. 138    18. 219    19. 153

Subtract 99 from each of these numbers.

20. 173    21. 249    22. 133    23. 387    24. 264

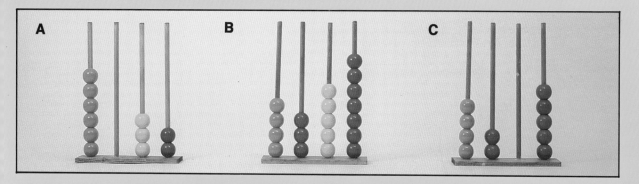

1. Which is the largest number?

2. Which is the smallest number?

3. Take 7 from C.

4. Add 14 to B.

5. Subtract 100 from A.

6. Find the total of B and C.

7. Find the difference between A and C.

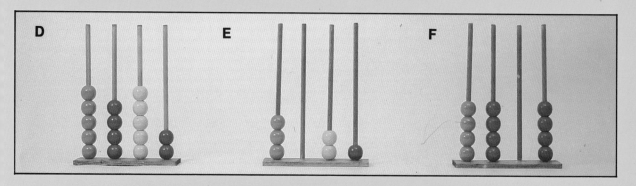

8. How many more than E is D?

9. What must you add to E to get 4000?

10. What must you take from F to get 1000?

1. Which gives the largest total?

   A   799
      + 4 9 9
      _____

      _____

   B   1 0 9 9
      +  2 3 8
      _____

      _____

   C   8 3 0
      + 5 1 6
      _____

      _____

   D   7 5 1
      + 5 4 9
      _____

      _____

2. Which pair of numbers has the smallest difference?

   A   1200 and 799         B   840 and 341

   C   1000 and 645         D   891 and 491

3. Which answer is nearest to one thousand?

   A   2 4 8
      ×    4
      _____

      _____

   B   1 1 2
      ×    5
      _____

      _____

   C    9 8
      ×   7
      _____

      _____

   D   2 6 0
      ×    6
      _____

      _____

4. Which gives the smallest answer?

   A  7⟌931      B  8⟌976      C  3⟌429      D  6⟌756

What is missing?

## What is missing here?

1.
```
   1 5
 + 2 *
 ─────
   3 8
```

2.
```
   2 7
 + * 2
 ─────
   5 9
```

3.
```
   4 1
 + 3 *
 ─────
   7 7
```

4.
```
   3 3
 + * 5
 ─────
   6 8
```

5.
```
   2 *
 + 4 5
 ─────
   6 8
```

6.
```
   * 7
 + 5 1
 ─────
   8 8
```

7.
```
   1 *
 + 3 7
 ─────
   4 9
```

8.
```
   * 8
 + 4 0
 ─────
   7 8
```

9.
```
   4 *
 − 2 7
 ─────
   1 5
```

10.
```
   5 4
 − 1 *
 ─────
   4 3
```

11.
```
   * 9
 − 2 *
 ─────
   1 2
```

12.
```
   4 *
 − * 7
 ─────
   2 6
```

Squared paper, isometric paper, pegboard, pegs

Use squared paper.
Draw a pattern of squares
increasing in size like this:

Continue the pattern until you
have drawn 6 squares.
Write how many small squares
there are in each square.

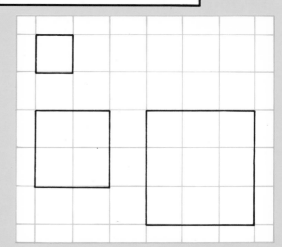

Use isometric paper.
Draw a pattern of triangles
increasing in size like this:

Continue the pattern until you
have drawn 7 triangles.
Write how many small triangles
there are in each triangle.

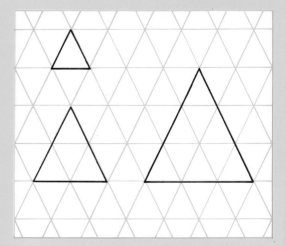

Use the pegboard.
Make a pattern of squares
increasing in size like this:

Continue as far as you can.
Write how many pegs there
are in each square.

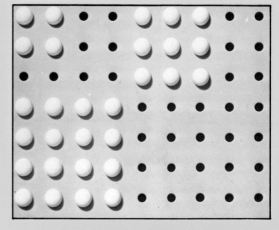

Use the pegboard.
Make this pattern.
Write how many pegs in the pattern.

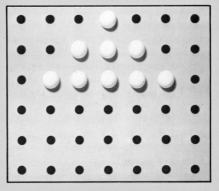

Add another row of pegs like this:
Write the number of pegs in
the pattern.
Continue the pattern adding a row
of pegs each time.
Write the total number of pegs
in each pattern.

The numbers 1, 4, 9, 16, 25, ...
are called **square numbers**.

You need a table square.
Colour in the square numbers.
What do you notice?

| × | 1 | 2 | 3 | 4 | 5 | 6 | 7 | 8 | 9 | 10 |
|---|---|---|---|---|---|---|---|---|---|---|
| 1 | 1 | 2 | 3 | 4 | 5 | 6 | 7 | 8 | 9 | 10 |
| 2 | 2 | 4 | 6 | 8 | 10 | 12 | 14 | 16 | 18 | 20 |
| 3 | 3 | 6 | 9 | 12 | 15 | 18 | 21 | 24 | 27 | 30 |
| 4 | 4 | 8 | 12 | 16 | 20 | 24 | 28 | 32 | 36 | 40 |
| 5 | 5 | 10 | 15 | 20 | 25 | 30 | 35 | 40 | 45 | 50 |
| 6 | 6 | 12 | 18 | 24 | 30 | 36 | 42 | 48 | 54 | 60 |
| 7 | 7 | 14 | 21 | 28 | 35 | 42 | 49 | 56 | 63 | 70 |
| 8 | 8 | 16 | 24 | 32 | 40 | 48 | 56 | 64 | 72 | 80 |
| 9 | 9 | 18 | 27 | 36 | 45 | 54 | 63 | 72 | 81 | 90 |
| 10 | 10 | 20 | 30 | 40 | 50 | 60 | 70 | 80 | 90 | 100 |

Make a number spiral
on squared paper.
Colour in the square
numbers.
What do you notice?

| | | | | | | | |
|---|---|---|---|---|---|---|---|
| | | | | | | | |
| | | | 10 | 11 | 12 | 13 | |
| | | | 9 | 2 | 3 | 14 | |
| | | | 8 | 1 | 4 | 15 | |
| | | | 7 | 6 | 5 | 16 | |
| | | | | | | 17 | |
| | | | | | | | |
| | | | | | | | |

9

# Measurement

Tape, trundle wheel

Remember: the total distance round a shape
is called a **perimeter**.

Estimate which of these shapes has the
largest perimeter.

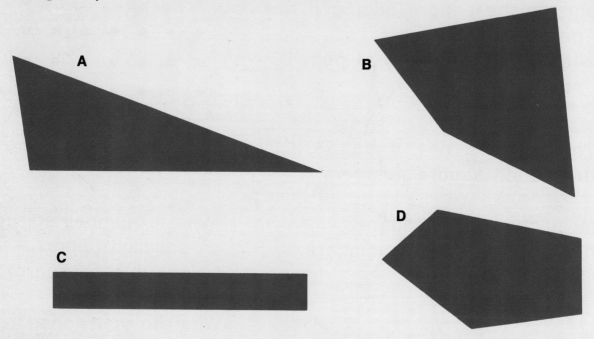

Now measure the perimeter of each shape.

Draw a triangle with a perimeter larger than 20 cm.

Measure the perimeter of this triangle.

Draw a square with the same perimeter.

Draw a square with the same perimeter as each of these.

The height of this man
is 1 m 79 cm.

You can write it as 1·79 m.

The height of his daughter
is 94 cm.

You can write it as 0·94 m.

The height of his son
is 1 m 8 cm.

You can write it as 1·08 m.

Copy this table and fill it in.

| | | |
|---|---|---|
| 240 cm | 2 m 40 cm | 2·40 m |
| 110 cm | | |
| 206 cm | | |
| | 3 m 26 cm | |
| | | 0·35 m |
| | | 1·64 m |
| 96 cm | | |
| | 1 m 5 cm | |

Trundle wheel or long tape, bean bags

## Who can throw further?

Ask a friend to help you.
Use either the hall or the playground.
Make a mark on the floor.
Each throw a bean bag from the mark.
Measure the length of each throw.
Find the difference between the lengths of the throws.

Do the same again.
Is the difference still the same?

Peter has 5 clockwork cars.
He wound up each car and let it go.

Car number 1 travelled 19·40 m.
Car number 2 travelled 15·80 m.
Car number 3 travelled 12·50 m.
Car number 4 travelled 10·80 m.
Car number 5 travelled  7·90 m.

Measurement

1.  Work out the distances between the cars when
    they stopped.

2.  Which two cars were closest when they stopped?

3.  How far was it from the first car to the last?

4.  Which car went twice as far as car number 5?

5.  How much further would car number 1 need to go to
    travel 20 m?

# Number

You can do these in your head, with a calculator or by working them out.

| 1. | 2. | 3. | 4. |
|---|---|---|---|
| $1999$ | $271$ | $900$ | $1000$ |
| $+\ \ 999$ | $+729$ | $-399$ | $-\ \ 401$ |

| 5. | 6. | 7. | 8. |
|---|---|---|---|
| $198$ | $999$ | $4\overline{)1004}$ | $3\overline{)2997}$ |
| $\times\ \ \ \ 5$ | $\times\ \ \ \ 6$ | | |

Find half of each of these.

9. 500     10. 1998     11. 5 m     12. £1·98     13. $1\frac{1}{2}$ l

Double each of these.

14. 699     15. 1499     16. £3·99     17. $2\frac{1}{4}$ kg     18. $1\frac{3}{4}$ m

19. $27 + 216 + 73$

20. Find the total of 296, 320 and 4.

21. Subtract 650 from 1649.

22. Find the difference between 884 and 442.

23. Multiply 121 by 10.

24. Divide 720 by 10.

Mr. Jackson is a postman.
He carries his letters in a postbag.
Some letters are first-class.
Some are second-class.

Yesterday he had 129 first-class
letters and 217 second-class
letters to deliver.

1. How many letters had he altogether?

2. In Richmond Road he delivered 24 first-class and
   37 second-class letters.
   How many letters were left in his postbag?

3. In the High Street he delivered 42 first-class and
   57 second-class letters.
   How many letters were left now?

4. When he had delivered letters in South Street, he
   had 94 left in his postbag.
   How many letters did he deliver in South Street?

5. In Long Close he delivered the 94 letters he had left.
   25 were first-class.
   How many were second-class?

These dials are from four different cars.

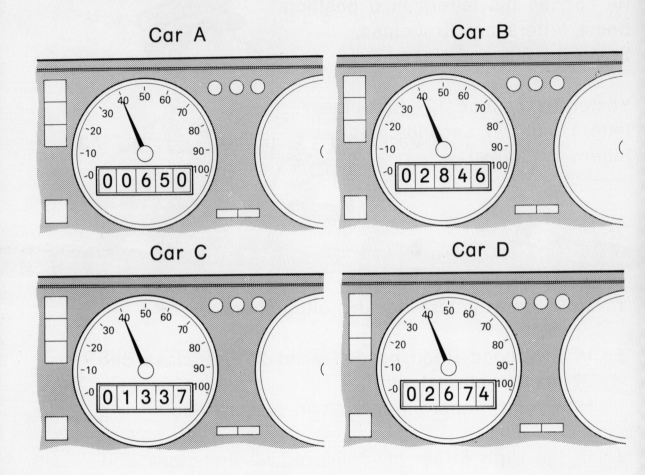

Car A   Car B

Car C   Car D

1. How many more miles before Car A reaches 1000?

2. How many more miles before Car B reaches 3000?

3. Car C travels 200 miles. What is its new reading?

4. Car D doubles its number of miles. What is the new reading?

5. How many more miles before the dial on Car D has two 4s in it?

## Reversing numbers

56 is a two digit number containing the digits 5 and 6.
247 is a three digit number containing the digits
2, 4 and 7.

| | |
|---|---|
| Write down any three digit number. The first digit must be at least 2 greater than the last digit. | 7 3 2 |
| Reverse the order of the digits. | − 2 3 7 |
| Find the difference between the two numbers. | 4 9 5 |
| Reverse the order of the digits. | + 5 9 4 |
| Add the two numbers. | 1 0 8 9 |

Now choose a three digit number of your own.

Reverse the digits and subtract.

Then reverse the digits and add.

What do you notice about your answer?

## Calculator

Make 100 on each calculator.
You can only use the keys shown.

**1.**

**2.**

**3.**

**4.**

**5.**

**6.**

## Calculator

The 3 key is broken.
Don't touch it!
Can you do these?

1. $32 + 54$

2. $29 + 93$

3. $49 \times 3$

4. $138 - 79$

5. $103 - 78$

6. $116 - 43$

7. $43 \times 9$

# Shape

Squared paper

How many different shapes can you make using 5 squares?

The squares must fit
side to side like this:

This is not allowed:

All the shapes must be different.
These shapes are really the same.
It is the same shape in a different position.

Now find all the different shapes you can using 5 squares.
Draw each shape on squared paper.
Each shape is called a pentomino.

Shape

Can you cover this square exactly using
some of your pentominoes?

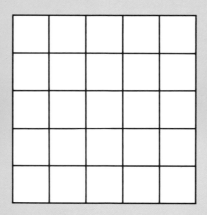

Can you cover this rectangle exactly using
all of your pentominoes?

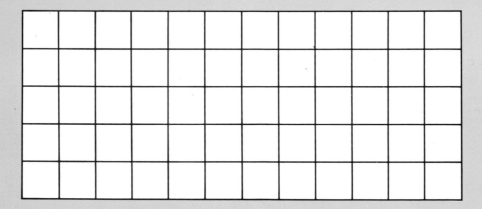

> 16 pin geoboard, elastic bands, spotty paper, mirror

These are all quadrilaterals.
Which ones have lines of symmetry?

Make as many different quadrilaterals on your
geoboard as you can.
Copy them on spotty paper.
Draw the lines of symmetry.

| 16 pin geoboard, elastic bands, spotty paper |
| --- |

These triangles and quadrilaterals have
right angles in them.

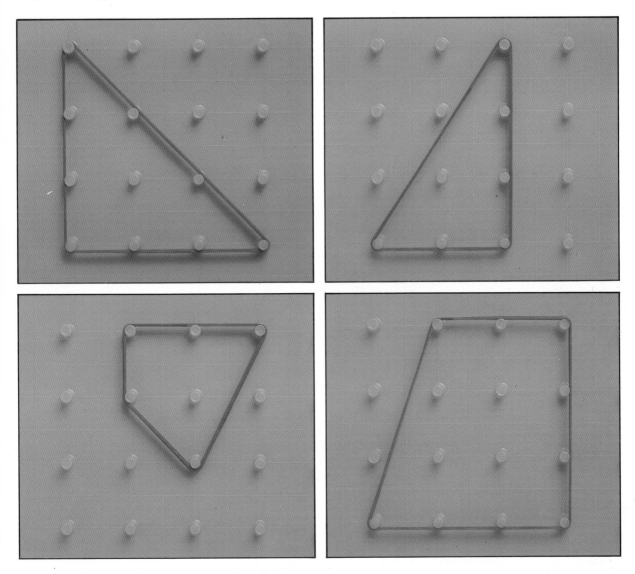

Make as many triangles and quadrilaterals with right angles
in them as you can.
Draw them on spotty paper.

| Interlocking shapes, squared paper |
| --- |

This cube is made
from squares.

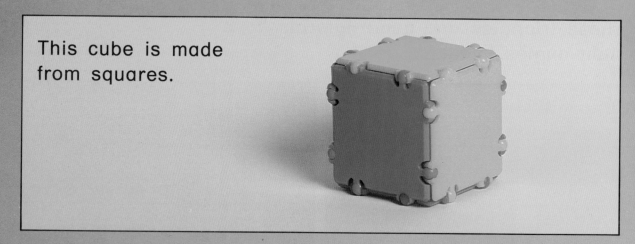

It can be undone to make this **net**.

Can you undo a cube to make other nets?

Make as many different nets as you can.

Draw each one on squared paper.

Card

Make 2 cubes from card.

You can write any digit on each face of the cubes.

How many different numbers can you make?

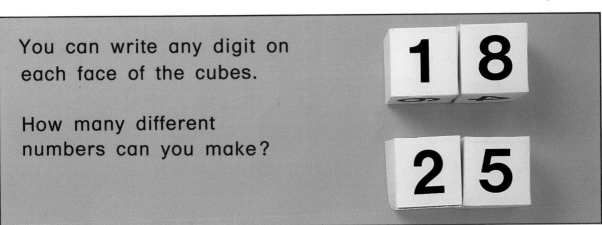

## Measurement

**Plane shapes**

This shape has two kinds of angle.

It has two angles less than a right angle, coloured green.

It has two angles greater than a right angle, coloured red.

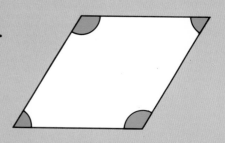

Draw round some shapes.

Colour green any angles less than a right angle.

Colour red any angles greater than a right angle.

Do not colour right angles.

## Plain paper

Make a $\frac{1}{2}$ right angle like this:

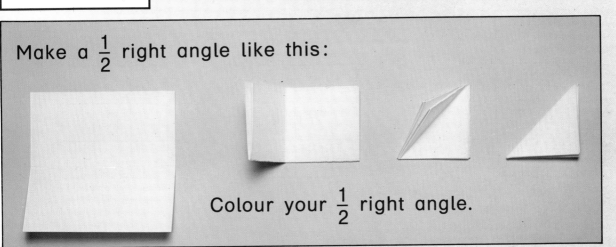

Colour your $\frac{1}{2}$ right angle.

Use your $\frac{1}{2}$ right angle to find if these angles are:

    less than $\frac{1}{2}$ right angle;

    greater than $\frac{1}{2}$ right angle;

    or $\frac{1}{2}$ right angle.

# Number

Each of these is part of a table square.
Fill in the missing numbers.

**1.**

| 21 |    | 27 |
|----|----|----|
|    | 32 |    |

**2.**

| 12 |    |    |
|----|----|----|
|    | 20 |    |
|    | 30 |    |

**3.**

| 3 |   |    |
|---|---|----|
|   | 8 |    |
|   |   | 15 |

**4.**

| 5  | 6  |    |
|----|----|----|
|    | 12 |    |
|    |    | 21 |
|    |    | 28 |
| 25 |    |    |

**5.**

|    |    |    |    | 48 |
|----|----|----|----|----|
|    |    |    |    |    |
| 32 |    | 48 | 56 |    |
|    |    |    |    | 72 |

**6.**

|    |    |    |    |
|----|----|----|----|
| 42 |    | 54 |    |
|    | 56 |    |    |
|    |    |    | 80 |

**7.**

|    |    | 16 |    |    |
|----|----|----|----|----|
|    |    |    |    |    |
|    |    | 24 |    |    |
|    |    |    |    |    |
|    |    | 32 |    |    |

**8.**

|    |    |    |
|----|----|----|
|    |    | 54 |
|    |    |    |
|    |    | 72 |

Multiply each of these by 10.

1. 76      2. 37      3. 48      4. 29      5. 160

6. 210      7. 400      8. 136      9. 101      10. 110

Divide each of these by 10.

11. 340      12. 170      13. 590      14. 1400      15. 1000

16. 2030      17. 1900      18. 3030      19. 2700      20. 5000

Each of these has a remainder.

Pair up the ones with the same remainder.

A  $10 \overline{)2713}$      B  $5 \overline{)429}$      C  $10 \overline{)6017}$

D  $5 \overline{)716}$      E  $10 \overline{)1648}$      F  $2 \overline{)361}$

G  $10 \overline{)3618}$      H  $5 \overline{)598}$      I  $10 \overline{)726}$

J  $5 \overline{)1314}$      K  $10 \overline{)1717}$      L  $10 \overline{)936}$

Calculator

This table square has three coloured rectangles.

Look at the green rectangle.

Multiply the numbers in the opposite corners.

Use your calculator to help you.

| 1 | 2 | 3 | 4 | 5 | 6 | 7 | 8 | 9 | 10 |
|---|---|---|---|---|---|---|---|---|---|
| 2 | 4 | 6 | 8 | 10 | 12 | 14 | 16 | 18 | 20 |
| 3 | 6 | 9 | 12 | 15 | 18 | 21 | 24 | 27 | 30 |
| 4 | 8 | 12 | 16 | 20 | 24 | 28 | 32 | 36 | 40 |
| 5 | 10 | 15 | 20 | 25 | 30 | 35 | 40 | 45 | 50 |
| 6 | 12 | 18 | 24 | 30 | 36 | 42 | 48 | 54 | 60 |
| 7 | 14 | 21 | 28 | 35 | 42 | 49 | 56 | 63 | 70 |
| 8 | 16 | 24 | 32 | 40 | 48 | 56 | 64 | 72 | 80 |
| 9 | 18 | 27 | 36 | 45 | 54 | 63 | 72 | 81 | 90 |
| 10 | 20 | 30 | 40 | 50 | 60 | 70 | 80 | 90 | 100 |

Now do the same with the other rectangles.

What do you notice?

Try it with other rectangles.

Now try it with a square.

Number

You can divide 10 by 1, 2, 5 and 10 without leaving any remainder.

You can show it like this:

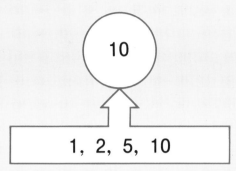

1. Can you finish this?

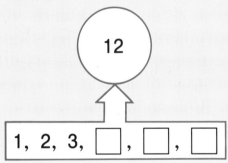

Show which numbers each of these can be divided by in the same way.

Remember there must be no remainders.

| | | | | |
|---|---|---|---|---|
| 2. 30 | 3. 27 | 4. 16 | 5. 36 | 6. 18 |
| 7. 32 | 8. 9 | 9. 15 | 10. 20 | 11. 14 |

Number

These table facts are hard to remember.
Do you know them all?

1. 8 × 6  2. 7 × 9  3. 8 × 7  4. 4 × 9
5. 9 × 6  6. 8 × 8  7. 7 × 6  8. 8 × 4
9. 7 × 7  10. 9 × 4  11. 7 × 9  12. 8 × 9
13. 6 × 6  14. 9 × 3  15. 9 × 9

Now do these.

16. Double 728.

17. Multiply 836 by 3.

18. 799 × 6

19. Multiply 10 and 5 and 7.

20. Which number is twice as great as 550?

21.  421
    ×   7

22.  936
    ×   8

23.  947
    ×  10

24.  592
    ×   6

25.  895
    ×   4

26.  676
    ×   3

27.  896
    ×   9

28.  761
    ×   5

34

Number

## Calculator

Find three numbers to multiply to make these answers.

Use your calculator to help you, if you need it.

**1.** 100

**2.** 60

**3.** 48

**4.** 54

**5.** 66

**6.** 108

Complete these.

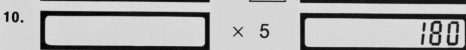

| Start | | Finish |
|---|---|---|
| **7.** 26 × ☐ | | 130 |
| **8.** ☐ × 6 | | 126 |
| **9.** 17 × ☐ | | 153 |
| **10.** ☐ × 5 | | 180 |

35

# Measurement

This bottle has been made into a measuring cylinder.

It measures in litres and millilitres.

1 l = 1000 ml

The reading on the bottle shows 1 l 400 ml.

It is written as 1·400 l.

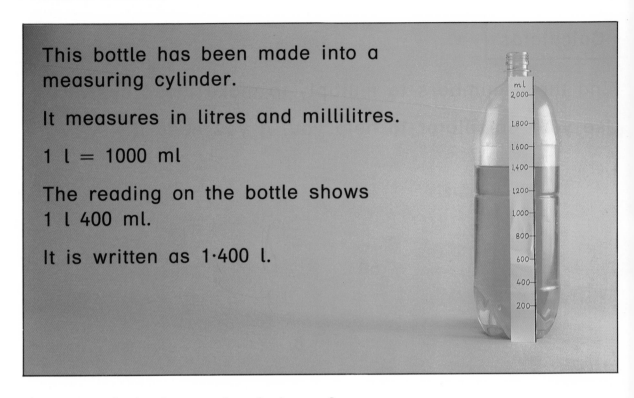

How much is in each of these?

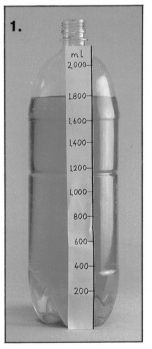

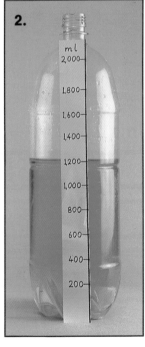

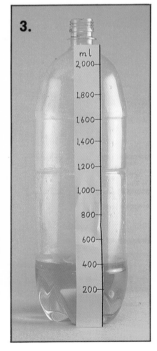

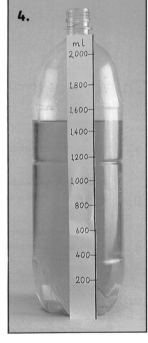

Mixing bowl, large jug, small jug, 2 l plastic bottle

Make a measuring cylinder from a plastic bottle.

Find containers like these.
Use your bottle to find out how much they hold.

# Number

5 gummed paper circles

**1.** Fold and cut the circle in half.

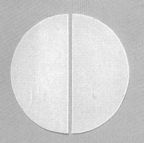

**2.** Fold one half in half. Cut along the fold.

**3.** Fold one quarter in half. Cut along the fold. Each piece is called an **eighth**. We write an eighth like this: $\frac{1}{8}$

**4.** Stick the pieces in your book. Label them like this:

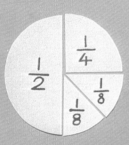

Fold and cut a circle into quarters. Label each piece $\frac{1}{4}$.

Fold and cut a circle into eighths. Label each piece $\frac{1}{8}$.

Stick the shapes in your book like this:

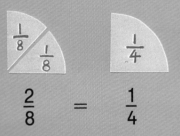

$$\frac{2}{8} = \frac{1}{4}$$

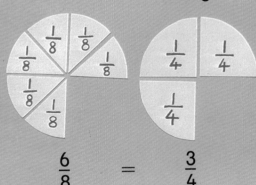

$$\frac{6}{8} = \frac{3}{4}$$

Fold and cut a circle in half. Label each piece $\frac{1}{2}$.

Fold and cut a circle into eighths. Label each piece $\frac{1}{8}$.

Stick the shapes in your book like this:

$$\frac{4}{8} \quad = \quad \frac{1}{2}$$

What fraction is coloured?

1.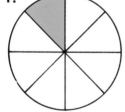

2.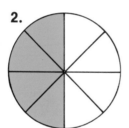

3.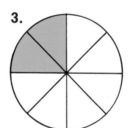

4.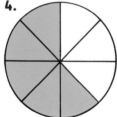

5.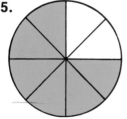

6.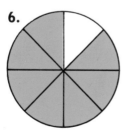

7.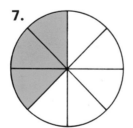

8.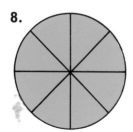

## Squared paper

Draw these shapes on squared paper.

1. Colour $\frac{1}{4}$ blue.

   Colour $\frac{1}{2}$ red.

2. Colour $\frac{3}{4}$ blue.

   Colour $\frac{1}{8}$ red.

3. Colour $\frac{3}{8}$ red.

   Colour $\frac{1}{8}$ blue.

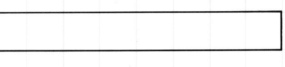

4. Colour $\frac{1}{4}$ blue.

   Colour $\frac{1}{8}$ red.

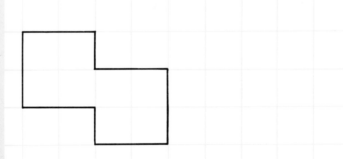

5. Colour $\frac{3}{8}$ blue.

   Colour $\frac{3}{8}$ red.

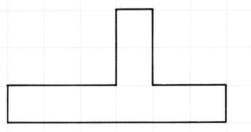

What fraction of each shape is coloured?

## Squared paper

This shape is divided into 5 equal parts.

Each part is $\frac{1}{5}$.

$\frac{1}{5}$ is coloured.

Draw these shapes on squared paper.

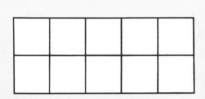

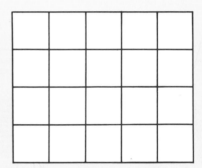

Colour $\frac{1}{5}$ of each shape blue.

What fraction of each shape is not coloured?

What fraction of these shapes is coloured?

1.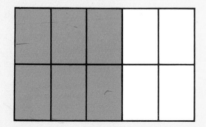

2.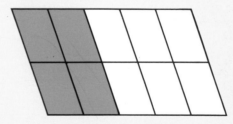

41

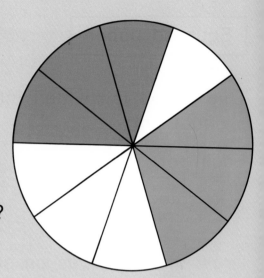

## Squared paper

This shape is divided into tenths.

Each part is $\frac{1}{10}$.

1. What fraction is coloured red?

2. What fraction is coloured blue?

3. What fraction is not coloured?

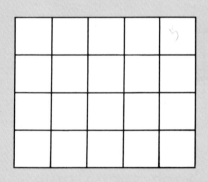

4. Cut out this shape.

   Colour $\frac{1}{2}$ red.

   Colour $\frac{1}{5}$ blue.

   Colour $\frac{1}{10}$ green.

   What fraction is not coloured?

Put in the missing numbers.

5. $\frac{1}{5} = \frac{*}{10}$    6. $\frac{2}{5} = \frac{*}{10}$    7. $\frac{3}{5} = \frac{*}{10}$

8. $\frac{4}{5} = \frac{*}{10}$    9. $\frac{1}{2} = \frac{*}{10}$

# What readings do the letters point to?

1.
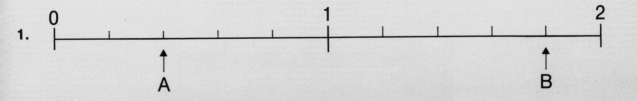

2.
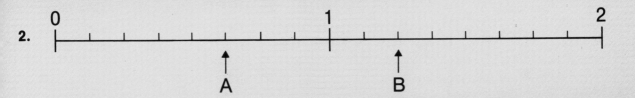

3.

4.

5.
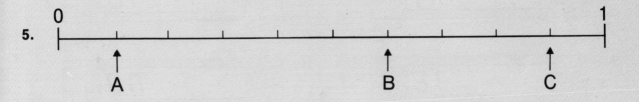

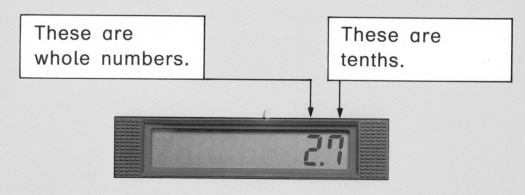

These are whole numbers.

These are tenths.

2·7 is a **decimal** number.

It is the same as $2\frac{7}{10}$.

Write these decimal numbers as fraction numbers.

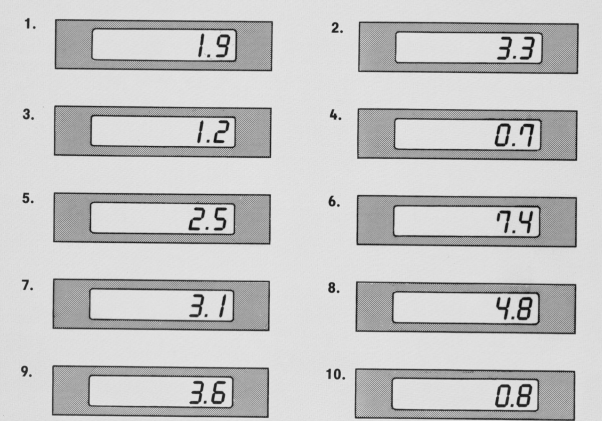

1.   1.9

2.   3.3

3.   1.2

4.   0.7

5.   2.5

6.   7.4

7.   3.1

8.   4.8

9.   3.6

10.   0.8

Number

1. What readings do the letters point to?

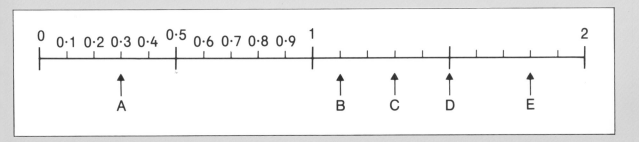

2. Which of these numbers
   are greater than $2\frac{1}{2}$?

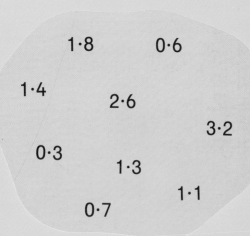

1·7      2·9

3·6

2·1                0·9

2·6           1·8

2·4

3. Which of these numbers
   are smaller than $1\frac{1}{2}$?

1·8        0·6

1·4
        2·6
                3·2
0·3
        1·3
             1·1
    0·7

# Measurement

These scales measure in kilograms and grams.

1 kg = 1000 g

The reading on the scales shows 1 kg 200 g.
It is written as 1·200 kg.

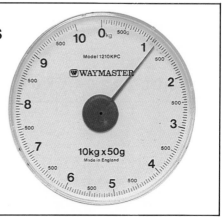

What do these show?

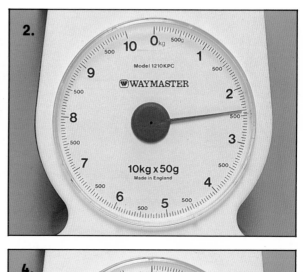

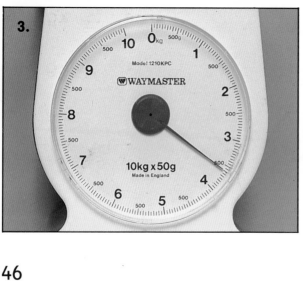

Write each of these weights in kilograms.

**1.** 1650 g

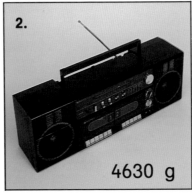

**2.** 4630 g

**3.** 2500 g

**4.** 3490 g

**5.** 2300 g

**6.** 1240 g

How many grams in each of these?

7. $\frac{1}{2}$ kg        8. $1\frac{1}{4}$ kg        9. $\frac{3}{4}$ kg        10. $2\frac{1}{2}$ kg

11. $1\frac{3}{4}$ kg        12. 2 kg        13. $2\frac{3}{4}$ kg        14. $3\frac{1}{2}$ kg

Find as many items that weigh
between 1 kg and 2 kg as you can.

# Number

Complete these:

**1.**
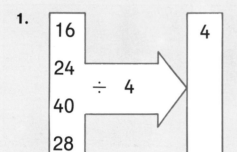

**2.**
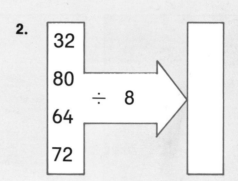

**3.** $4\overline{)404}$   **4.** $8\overline{)328}$   **5.** $5\overline{)735}$   **6.** $6\overline{)834}$

**7.** $10\overline{)620}$   **8.** $9\overline{)783}$   **9.** $7\overline{)973}$   **10.** $8\overline{)696}$

**11.** $4\overline{)364}$   **12.** $8\overline{)720}$   **13.** $7\overline{)637}$   **14.** $10\overline{)730}$

**15.** $\dfrac{78}{6}$   **16.** $\dfrac{65}{5}$   **17.** $\dfrac{84}{7}$   **18.** $\dfrac{96}{8}$

**19.** How many 9s in 468?   **20.** Find $\dfrac{1}{3}$ of 726.

**21.** $672 \div 8$   **22.** Find $\dfrac{1}{2}$ of 126.

**23.** Find $\dfrac{1}{4}$ of 204.   **24.** Find $\dfrac{1}{3}$ of 213.

**25.** Share 125 marbles equally among 5 children.

Number

1. Which give a remainder of 3 when you divide by 5?

   A  123    B  721    C  462    D  518    E  498

   F  620    G  519    H  313    I  628    J  343

2. Which give a remainder of 2 when you divide by 4?

   A  417    B  394    C  599    D  640    E  562

   F  802    G  475    H  381    I  578    J  364

Find the missing numbers.

3.  $8\overline{)40*}$ = 51

4.  $*\overline{)369}$ = 41

5.  $7\overline{)82*}$ = 118

6.  $4\overline{)41*}$ = *04

7.  $6\overline{)*96}$ = 66

8.  $5\overline{)35*}$ = 71

9.  $10\overline{)6*0}$ = 61

10.  $2\overline{)**6}$ = 223

11.  $\begin{array}{r} 3* \\ \times\ 5 \\ \hline 165 \end{array}$

12.  $\begin{array}{r} 10* \\ \times\ 3 \\ \hline 309 \end{array}$

13.  $\begin{array}{r} *7 \\ \times\ 4 \\ \hline 68 \end{array}$

14.  $\begin{array}{r} *14 \\ \times\ 6 \\ \hline 684 \end{array}$

## Calculator

Put each of these numbers on your display.
Add the smallest number you can to display 0 in the
tens column.
Record what you added for each one.

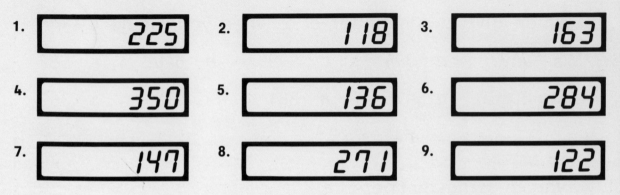

1. 225
2. 118
3. 163
4. 350
5. 136
6. 284
7. 147
8. 271
9. 122

Put each of these numbers on your display.
Multiply by the smallest number you can to display 0
in the units column.
Record what you multiplied by for each one.

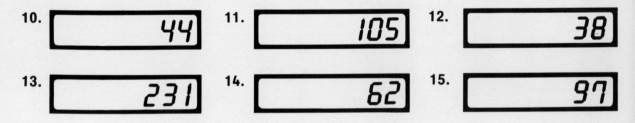

10. 44
11. 105
12. 38
13. 231
14. 62
15. 97

## Calculator, counters

### Cover the grid

A game for 2 players.

### Rules

Take it in turns to play.
Choose any pair of numbers from the
list opposite.
You can use either the $+$ or the $-$ key.
Is your answer on the grid below?
If so, cover it with a counter.
The winner is the first to get 4 counters
in a row.

| | |
|---|---|
| 64 | |
| 37 | |
| 29 | |
| 95 | |
| 48 | |
| 81 | |
| 52 | |
| 68 | |
| 73 | |

| | | | | |
|---|---|---|---|---|
| 112 | 8 | 110 | 143 | 31 |
| 35 | 176 | 120 | 44 | 132 |
| 93 | 101 | 66 | 27 | 121 |
| 47 | 159 | 52 | 85 | 124 |
| 168 | 149 | 141 | 125 | 19 |

# Measurement

cm squared paper

This is a 1 cm square.

Its area is 1 **square centimetre**.
We write it like this: 1 **cm²**.

The area of this shape is 7 cm².

Find the area of each of these shapes.

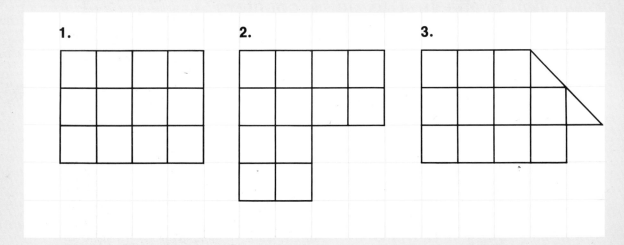

Draw some more shapes with the same area.

Measurement

# Find the areas of these shapes.

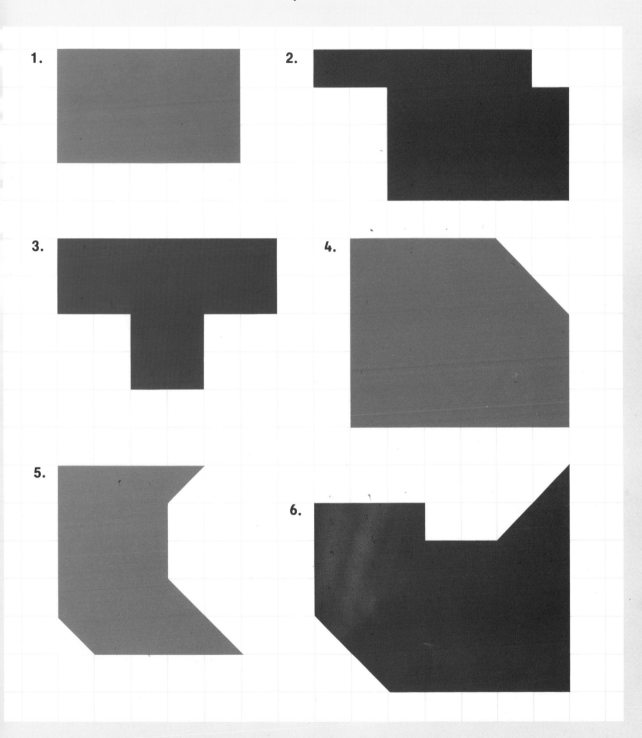

1.

2.

3.

4.

5.

6.

## Transparent cm squared grid

Look at each object.
Estimate its area.
Find its area using the transparent grid.
Record your results in a list.

| Object | Estimate | Area |
|--------|----------|------|
|        |          |      |

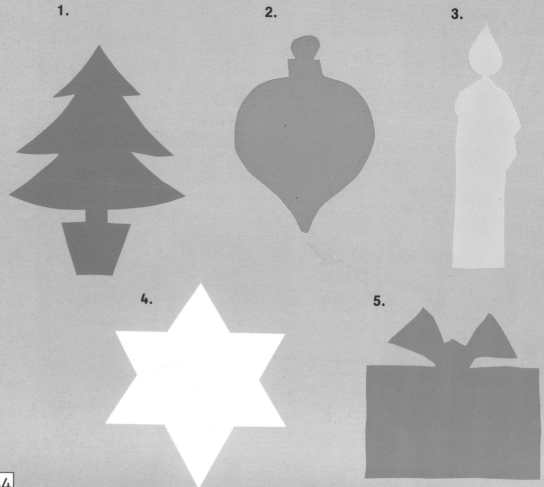

1.

2.

3.

4.

5.

Measurement.

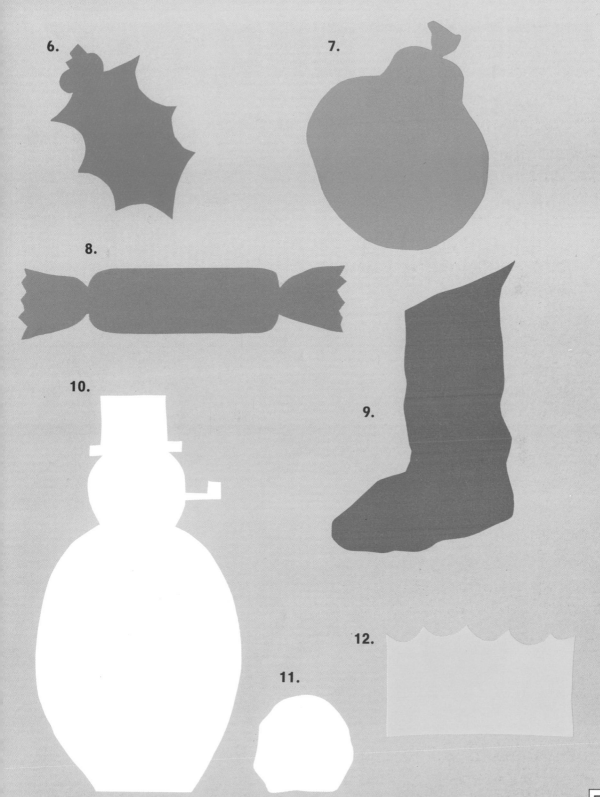

# Money

1. You can only use three stamps.
   Which amounts up to 20p can you make?

2. Which amounts up to 20p can you make if you use four stamps?

Joan Miles
26 River Way
Littleford
Berks
RG8 5GR

3. Use these coins.

Which amounts up to 50p cannot be made?

Money

1. Mr. Taylor has 4 children, all under 14.
   He decided to take his wife and children to York.
   How much did it cost him?

2. Mr. Selby has 3 children, aged 16, 10 and 9.
   He decided to take his wife and children to
   Blackpool.
   How much did it cost him?

3. Mrs. Martin has 3 children under 14.
   Her neighbour has 3 children under 14 as well.
   Mrs. Martin took the 6 children to Skegness.
   How much did it cost her?

4. Choose one of the trips for your family to go on.
   How much will it cost?

Blue paint      £1·75
White paint     £1·80
Yellow paint    £1·64
Green paint     £1·85

Mr. Watson is painting his house.

1. He needs 5 tins of blue paint.
   How much will they cost him?

2. He needs 6 tins of yellow paint.
   How much will they cost him?

3. He needs 3 tins of white paint.
   How much will they cost him?

4. He needs 4 tins of green paint.
   How much will they cost him?

5. How much will he spend on paint altogether?

Which bills come to more than £5?

**A** 2 bags of potatoes
1 tub of margarine
1 carton of ice cream
1 packet of butter

**B** 1 bottle of drink
2 bunches of bananas
2 tubs of margarine
1 carton of ice cream

**C** 2 tins of soup
2 bags of potatoes
2 bunches of bananas
2 tubs of margarine

**D** 4 tins of soup
1 bunch of bananas
1 carton of ice cream
2 bottles of drink

# Measurement

## Today's TV programmes

**1.00** News
**1.15** Cartoon Time: cartoon fun for children
**1.35** Under Fives: things for very young children
**1.45** Cricket: from Old Trafford, Manchester
**2.25** Film: Happy Days
**4.00** News
**4.15** Athletics
**5.00** In the Forest: a nature programme
**5.45** News
**6.30** Pop Scene: all the latest hits
**7.20** London Chimes: a programme about clocks in
London
**8.00** Gardening Today: looking at flowers

1. How long does the programme for under fives last?

2. How long does the afternoon film last?

3. Where is the cricket being played?

4. Which programme would a gardener want to watch?

5. Which programme lasts 20 minutes?

6. How long does the pop music programme last?

7. Which programme will tell you about clocks?

8. Which is the shortest programme?

Mr. and Mrs. Lewis have a son.
His name is David.
The postman called at their house.
There was no-one in.
Can you work out what time he called?

Mr. Lewis left home at 9.00 am
and came back at 4.30 pm.

Mrs. Lewis was out from 11.30 am
to 12.30 pm.

David went out with his friend
from 12 o'clock to 3 o'clock.

At which of these times did the postman call?

9.15, 11.45, 12.15, 2.30

# Write the time each of these shows.

1.

2.

3.

4.

5.

6.

7.

8.

9.

The alarm on each of these will ring at 8 o'clock.
How long before each alarm rings?

1.

2.

3.

4. CLOCK TIMER 6:20

5. CLOCK TIMER 6:55

6. CLOCK TIMER 6:40

The Wilsons have a meal at 5.15 pm.

7. The meat pie takes 45 minutes to cook.
   What time must it go in the oven?

8. The vegetables take 20 minutes
   to cook.
   What time must they go on
   the cooking ring?

9. The steamed pudding takes
   1 hour 40 minutes to cook.
   It was put on at 3.25 pm.
   Will it be done in time?

# Graphs and charts

This timetable is for buses from Exton to Manley.
The buses stop at Belton and Hadfield as well.

| Exton | 10.15 | 10.35 | 11.00 | 11.20 | 11.55 |
|---|---|---|---|---|---|
| Belton | 10.35 | 10.55 | 11.20 | 11.50 | 12.15 |
| Hadfield | 10.50 | 11.05 | 11.35 | 12.05 | 12.30 |
| Manley | 11.05 | 11.20 | 11.50 | 12.20 | 12.45 |

1. How many buses reach Manley before mid-day?

2. How long does the quickest journey from Exton to Manley take?

3. Which bus takes the longest time to do that journey?

4. Which bus gets to Belton at 11.50?

5. When does the 11.20 bus from Exton reach Hadfield?

| Calculator |
| --- |

Jenny's local football team is Norton Villa.
She goes with her brother and sister to watch them play.
This table shows how many people watched
their first six matches last season.

| Matches | 1st | 2nd | 3rd | 4th | 5th | 6th |
| --- | --- | --- | --- | --- | --- | --- |
| Number of people | 704 | 550 | 829 | 950 | 481 | 795 |

1. Which match had the largest crowd?

2. What was the difference between the largest crowd and the smallest?

3. At the second match, one-fifth of the crowd were children.
How many children were there?

4. At the third match there were 158 children.
How many adults were there?

5. What was the total attendance for the six matches?

This chart shows the weather for tomorrow.

1. Will it rain in Scotland?

2. What will the weather be like in Wales?

3. Will you need an umbrella in the south?

4. Will you need a coat on the east coast?

5. Where do you think the temperature will be lowest?

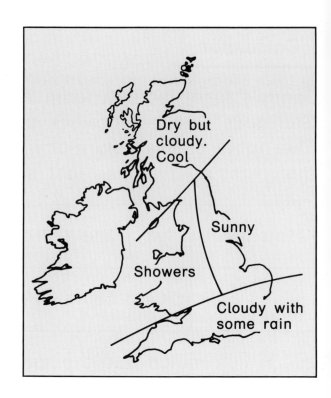

This chart shows the temperature in some cities yesterday.

6. Which city was warmest?

7. Which city was coldest?

8. Which other cities were as warm as London?

9. How much warmer than Edinburgh was Cardiff?

10. Which was the warmest place in Scotland?

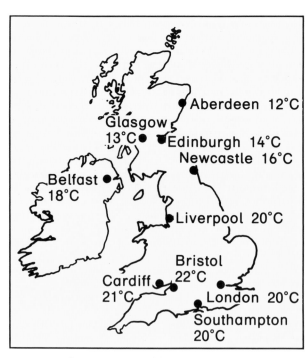

Graphs and charts

The weather at Burston-on-sea is usually good.
This graph shows the number of fine days there were
each month last year.

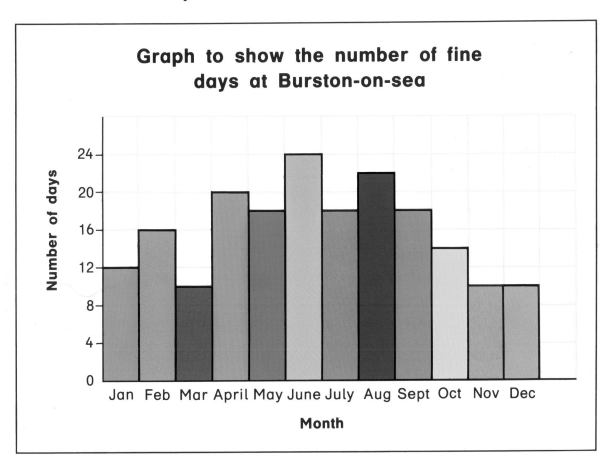

1. Which months had fewest fine days?

2. Which month had most fine days?

3. How many more fine days were there in June than in May?

4. On how many days in October was the weather
   not fine?

5. How many fine days were there altogether in the year?

# Assessment

1. Find the total of 2478, 49 and 3047.

2. Find the difference between 406 and 298.

Find the missing numbers:

3.
```
    1 * 6
  ×     3
  ───────
    3 1 8
  ───────
```

4.
```
    2 1 6
  − 1 * 5
  ───────
      3 1
  ───────
```

5.
```
         1 0 2
    5 ) * 1 0
```

6. What fraction is coloured?
   What fraction is not coloured?

7. $\frac{6}{8}$ is the same as ☐

What do these readings show?

8.

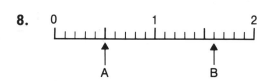

9.

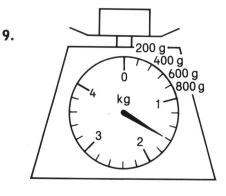

10. Which is greatest, $1\frac{1}{2}$ l, 1·300 l, 1·700 l?

Double each of these:

11. £2·99

12. $1\frac{3}{4}$ kg

13. 500

What is half of

14. 700

15. £3·02

16. $2\frac{1}{2}$ l

**17.** Find the perimeter of this shape.

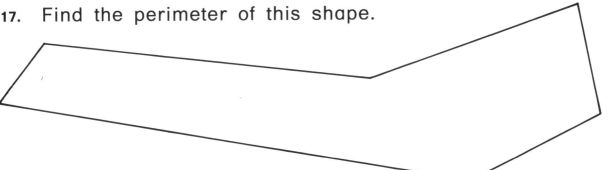

Write these as whole numbers and fractions:

**18.** 1·9          **19.** 2·2          **20.** 1·5

**21.** Which of these is greater than $3\frac{1}{2}$?
1·7, 4·8, 3·4

**22.** How many minutes from 1.30 pm to 2.15 pm?

**23.** What is the area of this shape?

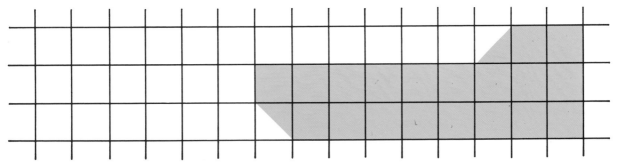

**24.** Draw a graph showing the following information about the people using a bus stop.

| Day | Sun | Mon | Tues | Wed | Thurs | Fri | Sat |
|---|---|---|---|---|---|---|---|
| Number of people | 250 | 550 | 600 | 500 | 400 | 850 | 900 |

# Glossary

**century**

a hundred

**decimal number**

a number which contains a decimal point (for example, 2·7)

**decimal point**

a point which separates whole numbers from fractions

**diagonal**

a line across a shape from one vertex to another

diagonal

**diameter**

a straight line through the centre of a circle

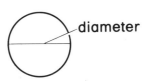
diameter

**digit**

a single number (from 0 to 9)

**gram (g)**

1000 g = 1 kg

**half right angle**

half a square corner

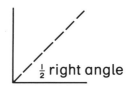
½ right angle

**hexagon**

any shape with 6 sides

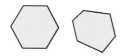

**key**

part of a calculator

key

**kilogram (kg)**

1 kg = 1000 g

**litre (l)**

1 l = 1000 ml

**millilitre**

1000 ml = 1 l

**net**

a shape which makes a solid when it is folded

**octagon**

any shape with 8 sides

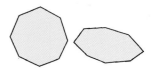

**pentagon**

any shape with 5 sides

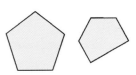

**pentomino**

a pentomino
is made
from 5
squares

**perimeter**

the distance
round a
shape or
object

**quadrilateral**

any shape
with 4 sides

**square centimetre**

a unit of
measurement
for area,
written as
cm²

**square number**

a square
number is
made by
multiplying
any number
by itself (for
example
$1 = 1 \times 1$,
$4 = 2 \times 2$,
$9 = 3 \times 3$)

**temperature**

how hot
or cold
something is.
Measured on
a thermometer.

**tessellate**

to fit shapes
together
without gaps

# Multiplication square

| 1 | 2 | 3 | 4 | 5 | 6 | 7 | 8 | 9 | 10 |
|---|---|---|---|---|---|---|---|---|----|
| 2 | 4 | 6 | 8 | 10 | 12 | 14 | 16 | 18 | 20 |
| 3 | 6 | 9 | 12 | 15 | 18 | 21 | 24 | 27 | 30 |
| 4 | 8 | 12 | 16 | 20 | 24 | 28 | 32 | 36 | 40 |
| 5 | 10 | 15 | 20 | 25 | 30 | 35 | 40 | 45 | 50 |
| 6 | 12 | 18 | 24 | 30 | 36 | 42 | 48 | 54 | 60 |
| 7 | 14 | 21 | 28 | 35 | 42 | 49 | 56 | 63 | 70 |
| 8 | 16 | 24 | 32 | 40 | 48 | 56 | 64 | 72 | 80 |
| 9 | 18 | 27 | 36 | 45 | 54 | 63 | 72 | 81 | 90 |
| 10 | 20 | 30 | 40 | 50 | 60 | 70 | 80 | 90 | 100 |